L.A.B.E.L.S

Strategies to Help Heal

Negative Thought Patterns

#NOMORELABELS

By,

VERNICE M. MITCHELL

*Published by,
Victorious Development
Louisville, KY*

L.A.B.E.L.S

Strategies to Help Heal Negative Thought Patterns

By, VERNICE M. MITCHELL

Copyright © 2018 by

All rights reserved. No part of this book may be reproduced or transmitted in any form or by any means without the express written permission of the publisher except for the use of brief quotation in a book review'

Printed in the United States of America

First Printing, 2018

ISBN 13: 978-1721164387

ISBN 10: 1721164383

Published by: Victorious Development LLC
              Louisville, Kentucky

Edited by: Niche with Words

LABELS

TABLE OF CONTENTS

Introduction: Labels Belong on Clothing...Not on Me! 1

Chapter One: Let Go (of the negative thoughts of others) 9

Chapter Two: Assess Your Life 20

Chapter Three: Be All You Can Be 29

Chapter Four: Establish Yourself 39

Chapter Five: Love Yourself 52

Chapter Six: Share 60

Chapter Seven: Renew, Relabel, Repackage 69

Introduction

Labels Belong on Clothing...Not on Me!

Labels are descriptive words or phrases used to place a person in a group or stereotype and can have either a negative or positive effect on an individual's life. Often labels are placed on a person during their childhood and are carried throughout the person's lifetime. Those labels can be buried deep down in the subconscious of the person's mind, unknowingly affecting the behavior of the person. Parents sometimes assign titles to their children out of anger and frustration. Those negative descriptions are etched into the brain of the child, and like a tape recorder on repeat, those negative descriptive words are played over and over in the mind, until the child believes the negative labels describe who they are or who they will become.

When negative labels are placed on a person, especially at a young age, it inevitably affects their self-esteem and self-worth. This then becomes a domino effect and spills out into each area of the person's life. The child that was labeled as LAZY because they were being a typical teenager by not keeping their room cleaned, now has the conversation in their mind that they are lazy. That title then becomes a crutch and can hinder the forward progression of the person. The "lazy" person rehearses the voice of their parent over and over in the mind stating that they are lazy, they then take ownership of that title. The voice of their parent now becomes their own voice because they have taken ownership of the label. The negative self-talk is constant throughout the persons day. Their daily routine includes thinking about the negative label that has been placed on them, whether it is a conscious or subconscious thought, it is always present.

I have always been a firm believer that we must be careful what we say around children, just as we have to be careful of the descriptive words that we use in describing a child. How many times have you heard someone call a child BAD or out of control because they do not know how to channel the energy that they have inside of them? Or the young person that is given the title of being HOT because her body is developing faster than her young mind can handle? And the child that is given the title of being LAZY and UNFOCUSED, yet they have not been introduced to anything that will stimulate their mind? Many times, the children who were labeled negatively, become teenagers and adults who end up living up to the negative descriptions. The negative self-talk, then becomes negative self-behavior. I know this to be true, because I was this child that was given negative labels, and those negative descriptions of me, followed me into my adulthood.

Not until I became an adult, did I realize the way I acted as a teenager, was a direct result of the labels that were placed on me as a child. I was a ten-year-old little girl and the label of being "hot and fast" was placed on me because my body was developing faster than I could understand. I was a ten-year-old child with the body of a teenager. My butt was huge, and my waist was small, which caused me to get unwanted attention from the opposite sex at such a young age. I was a child rapidly developing physically, but under developed in the mind. It was like my body was on super speed hormonally; at nine years old I started my menstrual cycle.

It was a day that will forever be etched in my brain. I recall going to the restroom to relieve myself and witnessing a massacre of blood in the toilet. I thought I was dying, I did not know what was going on. I was clueless to the fact that I had just started my menstrual cycle. I thought all of my organs were expelling out of my body. I recall screaming and calling out to my mom for her help. She rushed to the bathroom door and there I stood looking down at the toilet full of blood. "Momma, I'm bleeding. I'm dying," I said to her in a panic. My mother opened the door fully and explained, "Mechel, you are not dying! You are a woman now. You started your period. You know that packet that came in the mail the other day and you asked what it was? This is what it's for...your period." I was dumb founded, at the age of nine I had no clue as to what she was talking about. I thought to myself, "I'm a woman now?" I was puzzled as to what she meant by that. I just knew that I wanted this bleeding to stop, so I could go outside and have an acorn fight with my friends. I was not ready to be a woman. I was only in the 4th grade; now I'm a woman.

Soon after that fiasco in the bathroom, my mother got to the phone to tell everyone that, "Mechel, is a woman now. She started her period." I was still clueless and confused as to what was going on with my body, and what it was doing to me? No one had ever talked to me about a menstrual cycle and becoming a woman at the age of nine. I was so afraid of what was going to happen next. It was not until my sister came over to visit later that day, when I found out what it meant to have a menstrual cycle. She explained what was happening to me and what my mom meant by saying that I was a woman now.

At the age of eleven, my body was in full blown teenager form. I was drawing so much unwanted attention from boys. It was like they were buzzards circling around dead prey, waiting to swoop down on it. I was a tom boy by nature; I loved playing kickball and having acorn and water fights. I was a kid who just liked to have fun. My mother noticed all the attention that I was drawing, and this is when the labels started to flow more frequently. I was accused of having sex, even though I had no idea what sex was at the time. I was told that I was acting "hot" and was "smelling myself." I never really understood what that term "smelling myself" meant when I was younger. My early body development only made my mom become a lot stricter with me. I had become a prisoner in my own body, a little girl that developed way to fast and early, now, confused about herself and misunderstood.

Instead of having a discussion with me about what my body was going through, I was labeled and described to be someone that I was not. The power that a parent has in speaking life into their child is indescribable. My mom had already formed an evaluation of who I was, by how I looked externally, and the attention that my body was getting from the opposite sex. Instead of nurturing the child in me and giving me tools to use to allow me to truly know myself, I was labeled and sheltered. The teenaged me was not able to do much; I became the problem child because I had to sneak and do things with my friends. I would describe the teenaged me as opinionated. I recall times were I just wanted to be heard and given the opportunity to explain myself. I had one of those mothers who believed that children did not have a voice and did not need to be heard. I spent a lot of time alone in my room because I was always on a punishment.

One day, while on one of my many punishments, I decided that I would just live up to the label that had been placed on me, being "hot" and having sex. It was the summer going into my ninth-grade year of high school. It was not peer pressure that influenced my action, but a direct result of the label that had been placed on me. I figured that I might as well live up to what my mother had described me to be. Although, I was given the descriptive title of being "hot," I did not have multiple sexual partners in high school. I had one sexual partner, and with that sexual partner, I ended up pregnant at the age of sixteen.

Becoming a teenage mother was stressful and scary. I knew that I was about to face a challenge, I had no idea how to face. My child's father and I were not together. I knew that I was going to raise the child by myself. It was after I had my daughter when another label was placed on me by my mother..."alone." I was told that no man would ever want me or love me because I had a child. This conversation stuck with me and remained with me until my late twenties. My relationship with my ex-husband was a direct result of the conversation that was held with my mother. I was so happy that a man was showing interest in me and my child. I had defied her prediction that no one would want to be with me because I had a child. I felt like I had avoided the "alone" title. I had not become who she thought I would become; I was loved.

It was not until I was in my thirties, a divorced mother with three daughters, when I realized that the little girl in me was still carrying around the labels that had been placed on her as a child. I recognized that many of the choices that I made in life was a direct reflection of the negative self-talk from my childhood and teenage years. The negative descriptors that had been placed on the younger version of myself had followed me into adulthood. My mother and I had a strenuous relationship most of my adulthood, and this was not how I wanted our relationship to be. I needed a different connection with her. I prayed and asked God to show me how to heal from my past. Through prayer and meditation, I could help heal my inner child and remove the labels that had been placed on me as a child and teenager.

In this book, I will share the steps that I used to heal the hurt and remove the negative labels. In sharing my personal stories, I hope to help others who are carrying around negative labels. L.A.B.E.L.S. will give you tools that can be used to break the cycle of pain placed by negative descriptive words. You are not what others think of you, you are uniquely and wonderfully made. Release yourself from the negativity of your past and walk into the promise of a positive future. Now let's get to work on the healing process.

Chapter One

Let Go

(of the negative thoughts of others)

Negativity can be like a cancer that eats at the very core of your being. We sometimes allow negative people to pour their own toxicity and negative thought patterns into our own lives. The thoughts that people have about their own lives, can often subconsciously become our own thoughts about our individual lives, if we allow it to happen. Those thoughts then become self-talk, and the next thing you know, the negativity shows up in your behavior. Imagine a pendulum, you know, one of those ball things that hangs from a string. One ball hits the other, causing it to move, and that ball causes another ball to move. The negative label is the first ball, the next ball is our thoughts, and the last ball is our behavior. The movement back and forth started with the first ball, the negative label.

We can also think of it as a commercial that gets played at every commercial break. Have you ever watched a show, and half way through it you notice that the same commercial, let's say a cookie commercial, has been played several times already, and now you have the craving for chocolate cookies? The image of the chocolate chip cookies entered your mind subconsciously and placing the thought of cookies in your mind, triggering the craving for chocolate chip cookies. You were not thinking about eating cookies until the thought was planted in your mind by the commercial. That's how the negative thoughts and words of other's affect our own actions. That negative label that the person implanted in our mind stays with us and we carry it around until we start to believe it and our behavior follows the pattern of our thoughts.

    Growing up, I always wanted to become a nurse; I knew that I had the desire to help others in need. Before I became a teenaged mother, I planned on attending college and pursuing my nursing degree. But once I became a mother, my thoughts changed about my future. I knew that I had a baby to care for and wanted to finish high school. At the time, I had a job at one of the local grocery stores and was only making minimum wage. It was an ok job, and at least I was getting paid. I was told, by people who had a strong influence on my life, that I would probably never be able to become a nurse, since going to nursing school and having a baby would be too hard for me to do by myself. I was encouraged to just work and not focus on college after high school, because my priorities had changed. I believed the words that were told to me about my life path; I had accepted the label of "NO FUTURE." I felt stuck with no true picture of my own potential, so I settled for the one that was given to me.

Senior year of high school, many in my class were excited about college and their life plan. Meanwhile, I was feeling mundane about my own future, because I did not have a bright one. I made myself ok with the fact that I would just work a job, make money, get a check, and raise my daughter. That trajectory would be my future, since the seed that I could not attend college and have a child, because of the difficulty for me to do on my own. The thought of someone in my 'support system,' had become my own thought about my future. Instead of accepting the challenge of being a mom and attending college to brighten the future for us both, I laid down and accepted defeat without trying. My dream of becoming a nurse died with my thought process.

I had accepted the destiny that someone else had spoken over my life. I allowed the negative prediction to stagnate my life. That one seed planted in my mind, grew into a whole way of thinking for myself. I was not giving the 'other side of the coin' a positive outlook on my future. A future that include me attending school, going through some obstacles, developing a stronger 'support system' that would assist me in raising my child while I attended school. Instead, I was presented with the struggle. The negative outlook of how hard it would be going to classes, having to find a baby sitter, finding the time to study, while raising my child. I did realize that I had options and resources that would have helped me. I was frozen in my own fear of struggle. I wore that label like a badge of identity. I was afraid of the struggle before I even stepped into the battle.

During my early twenties, I was the mother of two daughters and in a relationship with my daughter's father. I knew that I had to have a job that would allow me to care for my children. While working as a cashier at the grocery store, and not making much money to support myself and my children, I had the desire to be more than a cashier. I made up my mind to go to school to do something in healthcare, but negative seed remained with me. I figured that since nursing school was going to be too hard for me to attend while raising one child, it was going to definitely be a struggle with two small children. So, I settled for a nine-month clinical medical assistant certificate program at one of the local schools. It was not a registered nurse degree, but it was a job that I could work and make money at for the rest of my life.

By this time, I had become a wife and was in a relationship where I literally lost myself trying to maintain. But I had accomplished the "American dream," the house, cars, a husband, and children all by the age of twenty-five. I had defied the prediction that my mother had spoken into my life. I was happy; I had my family. On paper things looked great, but my mind was a cesspool of negative thoughts and ideas, about myself and my future. I needed more out of life than what I was doing at the time. The desire to become a nurse would not leave my thoughts. The small whisper would become a loud yelling voice telling me that I needed to become a nurse, but how would I do it now that I had a husband, two children and pregnant with our third child?

At the time, it was not easy presenting the idea of going to school to become a nurse to my husband. He was not a fan of the idea of creating more debt, and the time it would take away from our family while I attended school. I was reminded again of how hard it would be to attend school, while raising three children and having my husband's needs to attend too. I was devastated. I thought to myself, "Here I go again with the negativity from my support system." It was overwhelming, and this time it was my husband. So, I settled in my mind that there would be no way for me to attend college without his support. I was about to rest in that negative thought process and allow the someone else's perceived fear, to control my destiny. I was about to bury my dream of becoming a nurse, when one of my daughters asked me, what it was I dreamt of becoming when I was little girl, and I said a nurse. And then she went on to ask me why I did not become a nurse when I grew up.

I was dumbfounded. I had no real answer for her. What was I supposed to say to my little girl? Was I supposed to tell her that someone advised me that it would be too hard to attend college with a child by myself? It was at that moment, while looking down into my daughter's eyes, that I knew it was either now or never for me to follow my dreams, and not allow fear of the unknown struggle to hinder my future. So, at the age of twenty-seven years old, the mother of two and pregnant with the third, and without the emotional and mental support of my husband, I enrolled in school to become a Registered Nurse.

Over the years, I have thought to myself... "What if I had never allowed the negative thoughts of others to be implanted into my own thought process after high school? Where would be? How far would have gone in life?" When my daughter asked me what I dreamt of being when I grew up, I was not expecting that question to move me like it did at the time. I decided at that very moment, to let go of the negative thoughts that others had placed on my life. I was determined not to allow the thoughts of others, to determine my future. Yes, it would be hard to attend college married, with children, handling life and all that comes with it. But, it was even harder to answer my daughter's question, and actually say out loud that I wanted to become a nurse. Then, to have to explain to her why I had not pursued this goal. I know that I had to go the route that I went, to build the confidence to pursue my dreams.

The many years of negative self-talk and negativity from my support system was engrained into my very being. It was a part of me.

Once I made the decision that I was going to follow my dreams no matter what, I had to go through the process of retraining my mind to think differently about my ability, and ask myself, was I willing to go through the struggle? Was my goal of becoming a nurse, bigger than my fear of struggling through school, trying to balance all that I had on my plate? And at the time, the answer was, I was unsure. All I knew, was that I had to change my thoughts, in order to change my life's path. I had to let go of the label of fear.

Sometimes we are not aware that we are taking on the negative thoughts of others, when it concerns our own life. It can be hidden as good advice from someone that is genuinely attempting to help. The person could be giving sound advice, but the negativity comes when it alters the forward progression in your very own life. The simple advice, that going to college and raising a child would be a hard task for me to do, became a way of thinking for me throughout my early adult life. I became trapped by the thought of struggle. I took on the negative thought of someone else, and that thought was like a bad seed planted in the soil; I would never produce good fruit.

Once we recognize that our thoughts about our life have become negative, we must develop a way to let go of those negative thoughts that we have internalized. The process of letting go of the label, of the 'fear of struggle,' involved lots of self-discovery. Just like the labels that were placed on me as a child, this label was placed by someone close to me. As a young mother, I looked to others for guidance and support in the decisions that I had to make in life. I had become who they said I would be, someone that was afraid of struggling. But little did I know that I would discover my own strength in the struggle of balancing all my roles while attending college. If I had known myself, when I was told about the struggles of attending college with a child, I would have been able to appreciate the advice, but not internalize and accept it has my own fate.

The process of letting go of labels can be difficult depending on how long you have worn the label and rehearsed the negative thought in your mind. After discovering who you are through self-discovery, replace those negative thoughts with positive ones, with positive self-talk. Implementing daily positive affirmations into our life, aids in removing the negative self-talk, ultimately helping to decrease the reoccurrence of the negative thoughts. In letting go of the negative thoughts placed in our lives by others, we can discover our own life path. Letting go of the negativity allows growth. It is like pruning dead branches from a tree, growth happens when we remove dead things from our lives. The negative thoughts of others, that we allow to affect our own lives, are the dead branches that need to be pruned for you (the tree), to fully grow. Let go of the negative thoughts in your mind placed by someone else, so that you can grow and develop into who God originally wanted you to be.

Reflections

Chapter Two

Assess Your Life

Once we have recognized that we have identified ourselves with labels placed by someone else, it is important that we learn who we truly are and replace those negative labels (thoughts) with positive ones. One way of looking into our life to gain a better understanding, is to perform an assessment of our lives. When we assess our life, it is best to evaluate every aspect of it. While having our mental, physical, emotional and spiritual life in mind, ask yourself the question, "Have I allowed negative thoughts to hinder my growth in this particular area of my life?" This self-assessment will require you to be honest with yourself. It will require transparency with the one person that is unavoidable, YOU. Taking a true evaluation of yourself in each area will help identify the area of need. Self-evaluation allows us to understand and know ourselves fully. This assessment will become a tool to assist in identifying the negative labels that have been placed on us by others.

I was not a perfect teenager, but I would say that I was a typical one. As a teenager, I told my fair share of little white lies to get my mom to say yes to something that I wanted to do. For example, I would ask to spend the night over my best friend's house so that I could go skating with her and hang out with my friends. I knew that my mother would never let me go. She was not one of those parents that allowed her teenaged daughter to attend the teen parties, but I was the teen that wanted to hang with my friends. I had to stretch the truth or sometimes leave part of it out, to be able to do things with my friends. I continued to stretch the truth or leave parts out knowing that my mom would find out the truth every time. After she would find out the truth, the name calling would begin. My mom would be furious when she found out and say, "you are a liar; there is no way that I will ever believe anything you tell me." And then, I would be on another punishment. I was in trouble a lot as a preteen and teen. I was the girl that had to stay on the porch and could not go outside of the gate that was around the yard. I was trapped in my own house because I was always in trouble. And whenever I would get in trouble, I would be called a liar, and told that she would never believe anything I said. She would say things like,

L.A.B.E.L.S   21

"How could anyone believe anything that comes out of your mouth, you do not tell the truth." It was not that I enjoyed keeping things from my mom, it was that I just wanted to do what the other teenagers were doing. I knew, that the only reason that I would stretch the truth was because I wanted to hang with my friends and be a teenager.

I would never tell a story just for the sake of telling one. I felt that she would never let me do anything simply out of fear that something would happen to me. She was just parenting me the best way she knew how, but the label that was placed on me remained attached to my inner self. I knew that I was not a liar, but I did replay the voice of my mother over and over, affirming that no one would ever believe anything that came out of my mouth.

Although, I do not believe that my mom said those words with the intentions that I would carry them around with me for majority of my life, those words followed me for many years. I had internalized that one label and it transformed the way I operated in life. I became an adult who felt I had to prove to people that I was trust worthy. I would go out of my way to show and prove my trustworthiness to people. In my mind, I felt people did not believe me, even though I had done nothing to make them think I was dishonest. This way of thinking became exhausting to me. I was walking through life allowing the negative label placed on me as child, to lower my self-esteem, and control the way I approached connecting with other people.

As a nurse, I perform assessments on patients that I care for on a regular basis. The assessment begins at the first encounter with the patient, as soon as I see them. I assess their appearance, what they are doing at the time, the condition of their skin, and the expression on their face, before I say one word to them. I monitor their behavior, and I ask general questions to evaluate the persons level of understanding and mental state. I listen to their heart, lungs, and abdominal sounds, and measure the strength of their extremities. This assessment helps the healthcare provider identify the area of the patient's health that may be deficient and is an aid in treatment and diagnosing the medical issue.

Maybe, you have had a loved one in the hospital or you have been hospitalized yourself, think back to that experience. The nurse performs their assessment by asking a series of questions, vital signs are checked and monitored, the nurse listens to the patient's heart and breathing while observing the actions of the patient. The series of questions asked, assists in identifying the area possibly causing the patient's illness. The answers to the questions are reported back to the healthcare provider to aid in the diagnosis and treatment of the illness. The assessment performed by a nurse is similar to the one that you will perform on yourself. You will have to take a close look at yourself and answer some difficult questions. Asking yourself these questions may have you feeling uncomfortable, but the goal is to get down to the root cause of it all and began the healing process.

In answering these questions, I was required to be transparent and honest with myself. I had to have an open mind and allow God to reveal the areas where the negative labels had embedded themselves in my thought process, about myself. Performing the assessment also allowed me to discover where the negative labels originated. In prayer, I asked God to help me ask the right questions in the assessment of myself. I had a serious talk with God. I talk to God as if I were talking to one of my friends. I knew that God would reveal to me the negative thoughts I had about myself and assist me in replacing those negative thoughts with positive.

To perform the assessment, we must take a close look at ourselves, LITERALLY. This will require a mirror...Go ahead get in front of the mirror! I am serious…really, get in front of the mirror and ask yourself the following questions. What do you see when you first lay eyes on yourself? What thoughts do you have when you see yourself in the mirror? What do you say to yourself when you look in the mirror? Are your thoughts about yourself negative or positive? If you have a negative thought, what are they? Where do you think those negative thoughts originated? Were they self-imposed labels or labels that were placed on you early in life? How have those negative thoughts about yourself affected your life? Do you feel like the thoughts have hindered your personal growth?

When I looked in the mirror, I saw someone who was not representing themselves as they truly are, and I allowed someone else's idea of me to represent who I was at the time. When I performed the assessment, and asked myself the mirror questions, I had blonde hair, and I did not even want to have blonde hair at the time. My beautician talked me into doing something "different" to my hair, so I allowed her to color it blonde. I received lots of compliments and I enjoyed receiving each one, but deep down inside I really didn't feel comfortable with my appearance. I was basically being someone that I was not. A simple change in my hair color allowed me to reflect on my childhood, when I was accused of being someone that I was not. Instead of being strong enough to tell my beautician that I did not want to have my hair color changed, I went along with it and became the image that she saw me as at the time. This was the same thing that I did when I was younger. I was accused of doing things that I was not doing, so I started to do the things, since I was being accused of it anyway.

It was difficult to confront myself about myself, but I went through all the questions one by one and wrote each answer down. Writing my answers down on paper gave me the opportunity to see my thoughts in words. Once I had them written down on paper, like the nurse does with their assessment, I took my answers to the GREAT physician...GOD! Through prayer, meditation, and conversations with Godly counsel I could finally begin the healing process.

The assessment reflects yourself in words. The goal is to identify where thoughts about yourself have been impacted by the negative labels. Just like a nurse that assesses a patient, the time needed for the assessment may vary from person to person. For some, performing the assessment may be a quick process and for others it may take some time. It all depends on how deep we have allowed the negativity to barrow down in our psyche and how open we are to reveal our inner most thoughts to ourselves. In revealing these negative thoughts, the desired outcome is healing. Sometimes in healthcare, a diagnosis may require a specialty provider to be consulted to assist in the treatment of the illness. And for some, the assessment may raise emotions and feelings that may require specially trained providers to assist with the healing process, and that is okay! So, if your assessment of yourself brings up thoughts and feelings that you cannot handle alone, seek out a local professional for a consultation. There is nothing wrong with talking to a professional about your thoughts and feelings. Remember, the goal is healing!

❧Reflections❧

Chapter Three

Be All You Can Be

Negative labels do not always come from someone else. We can often times attach negative labels on ourselves. We look at images on tv or social media and define ourselves by the images that we see on the screen. We can also attach negative labels to ourselves be comparing our own life to the lives of others. By doing this, we can think negatively about our own life because we are measuring our own success against someone else's measuring stick. Negative labels can also be formed from the words of a peer. Children being mean on the playground by calling another classmate a name can attach to the child being called the name for a lifetime.

Growing up one negative thought that I had about myself was that I was conceived by accident. My parents were not married at the time of my birth and I knew that the circumstances surrounding my birth were complicated. It could really be an episode of one of the reality shows that are on tv. I recall a time when I was in elementary school and one of my classmates called me a bastard. I had no idea what a bastard was, but I did know that I didn't feel good about myself when I heard the word come out of my classmate's mouth. I had to be in second or third grade. I was old enough to look the word up to find out the definition. And what I found was not a good definition. The dictionary stated that a bastard was a child born to unmarried parents. Another definition of a bastard was an unpleasant person. I thought to myself my parents were not married when I was born, so this must be me. At that moment I attached that definition to myself; I was a bastard, a despicable person. I allowed this one word to alter the way I thought about myself. As a young child, I had determined my own future. I had accepted the label that was placed on me and really thought that I was a bastard and unworthy.

I secretly wore the negative self-made label like a name badge that said who I was on my shirt. It was not until years later, I told my friend what I had learned about myself as a child, in the definition of the word bastard. We were both young and both born to parents who were not married when they had us. When I told her the definition and explained to her that I was a bastard, she became upset with me. She said to me, "If you are a bastard then I am a bastard...and I am NOT an unworthy person and you are not either." She looked at me and asked if I thought she was an unworthy person. Of course, I did not think that of one of my closest friends, so I told her "no." She simply said, "Then, stop calling yourself a bastard."

Once I realized that I had allowed negative labels to directly affect my way of living and thoughts about myself, I had to become the person that God designed me to be. The process of shedding old ways of thinking has been a trying task, because as soon as I think that I have rid myself of the negativity, the thoughts seem to creep their way back into my mind. The process of renewed thinking is a continual process for some, including me. I am forever evolving into my God given identity.

Someone once asked me the question, "Who are you?" I was excited because I thought I knew the answer to that simple question immediately when the person asked me. My response was, "I am a mother, a daughter, a sister, a friend, and a nurse." I was confident in my answer because I truly believed that those were descriptive words that describe me as God's creation. She asked me if I chose the correct words to describe myself and who I am. She wanted to know my characteristics. I paused and thought about each word that I used and I noticed each were titles and not descriptions of who I am. I truly thought the titles that I wore with pride described me as a person. I believed that was who I was, and now I had to be who God says that I am.

At this point, I was on a quest answer the question that my friend asked me, "Who am I?" I did not want to know myself as titles that I proudly wore. I was not created just to be those titles, I was created for more. I had to seek God to help me discover myself. One day while studying the bible, my identity became clearer to me. As a believer in Christ, I believe that my identity is in Jesus Christ. The characteristics that Christ represents are the same characteristics that we have as believers. I discovered that I had to be all that I could be in Christ. As a follower of Christ, the bible is my life guide, basically my compass and map to find direction in life.

In studying the bible, I knew that God would reveal who I am, because God knows me. Jeremiah 1:5 states, "Before I formed you in the womb I knew you, and before you were born I consecrated you..." reading those words allowed me to view myself differently. I knew that I would find my own characteristics while discovering who Christ is for myself. In Romans 8:29, the word states, "Those God foreknew he also predestined to be conformed to the image of his Son..." Therefore, I am predestined to emerge into the image of Christ my Savior.

Developing the character of Christ allows us to handle life situations more fluently. God places us in circumstances that will allow us to build Christ-like characteristics. I believe that the characteristics of Christ can be found in Galatians 5:22-23, which states, "But the fruit of the Spirit is love, joy, peace, forbearance, kindness, goodness, faithfulness, gentleness and self-control..." The fruit of the Spirit is a perfect description of the character of Christ, and it should be the goal of every believer, to become more like Christ and bear the fruit of Spirit.

Cultivating the characteristics of Christ starts in the mind, in the way we view ourselves. The negative labels that we wear can be direct obstacle to us becoming all that we can be in life. When we rehearse the negative thoughts in our mind about ourselves we do not give room to develop the Christ-like characteristics. This hinders our personal spiritual growth and blocks the blessings that are attached to the growth.

I developed an intentional plan to build my relationship with God. It took me some time to develop a routine that consisted of prayer, mediation, reading devotionals and immersing myself in the word of God. I must be honest and say, that I did not go gung ho and began all of this at once. It was a process that I developed a routine around. I started off with reading scripture and memorizing verses to recite to myself throughout the day. Then I began to meditate and sit silently to allow the Spirit of God, to fine tune my spirit. I incorporated daily devotional as a way of getting a better understanding of how to utilize the word in my daily life. Studying scripture helped expose those negative traits in myself and the relationships that I had with others.

My father and I have had an on and off relationship throughout my life. It wasn't like he was not there for me but we just did not consistently communicate with each other. There would be periods in our relationship when we would go months and many times years without communicating with each other. I kept up with him through family members, and from time to time we would talk briefly. Our relationship was this way not because we were angry at each other, it is just the way it was, and I had settled in my mind that our relationship would remain that way for the rest of our lives. I knew that I did not want our relationship to remain in the condition that it had been in over the many years. When my dad and I did talk he always gave me a word from God and a scripture. As a child, I recall that it was my dad who introduced me to Christ and allowed me the opportunity of salvation. But also, as a child, it was my dad who showed me that a man could hurt me without placing a hand on me, just by not being present as I needed. I was torn. I needed the word that God had placed in my dad to give to me, but I also held on to the hurt and pain of him not being in my life consistently. I carried the unwanted label around, not only because of what my mom previously told me, but also because the first man that I ever loved was not there for me, the way that I needed him to be. This was a place in my heart that only God would be able to heal.

In prayer, I cried out to God to heal my heart towards my dad, so that I could move on. I did not pray for God to heal our relationship, but I wanted my heart to be healed from the pain of rejection and abandonment. It was not an overnight process. It was a slow agonizing one that only God could see me through. I was open to the process and I can say that the relationship between me and my dad has been reconciled. God healed the heart of the nine-year-old little girl inside of me that missed her daddy. It took over thirty years for the process to show itself, to be a motion for healing, but this was all a part of the plan of me becoming all that I can be.

Now I know who I am when asked the question, "Who are you?" I can boldly answer, "I am an encourager, I am faithful, I am love, I am kind, and I am a peace-maker." I know that I have a long way in this journey of life to develop more Christ-like characteristics. I am determined to be all that I can be and build upon what has been deposited in me. As we grow on a personal and spiritual level, we develop more characteristics that aid us in becoming all that we can be.

Now the question to ask yourself is, "Who are you?"

❧Reflections❧

Chapter Four

Establish Yourself

Many of the negative thoughts that we have about ourselves are a direct result of our childhood experiences, but often, negative labels are placed on us as adults by our own doing. It becomes easy to observe the life of the next person and determine that we are somehow behind the curve because we do not have the money, house, car or life that someone else has at the time. As stated in the last chapter, what we view on television and social media can cause us to think negatively about our own lives. When we compare ourselves to others or pay attention to the next person's life, we can cause negative feelings about ourselves to develop. Those negative feelings become thoughts and those thoughts become labels that we attach to ourselves.

Thinking back to when my marriage ended, the fact that my marital status was changing, was devastating to me at the time. I was embarrassed when I had to check divorced on any application. I wore the title "DIVORCED" like a red scarlet letter around my neck. I had placed the labels of failure and shame on myself. On the outside, I seemed like I had it all together; I was frontin' and fakin! Inside I was a mess; the negative self-talk was at an all-time high. Every negative thought that I had ever thought of myself, was rehearsed in my mind throughout the day. I had convinced myself that I was not worthy of love or to have a man of my own. I reverted to the seventeen-year-old girl that was told over and over, that no man would ever want to be with her because she had a child. The shame and feeling of failure because my marriage ended was heavy and tiring, but I carried it around secretly for many years.

It wasn't until one of my daughters approached me with love, and proudly announced that she was proud of me and looked to me as her role model, when I realized that I never should have been ashamed of my marital status. Heck, fifty percent of Americans have been divorced, so why was I ashamed? We were not living in times where divorce was a taboo occurrence. I associated the end of my relationship with my ex, as a personal failure, and wore the label of shame because my marriage ended. I had so much to be thankful for and nothing to be ashamed of in my life. I had to mourn my old life and accept myself for who I was and where I was at the time.

My daughter's words were energy that jolted me into thinking about my reality. I recognized the fact that my daughters were observing me and coming to their own conclusion of who I was in their eyes. I always wanted the three of them to know, feel and understand my love for them. At that instant, I knew that I had to establish myself. The dictionary defines establish as "achieving permanent acceptance or recognition for." I had to permanently accept myself. Not just part of my life, but all of it. Life was going to happen and I could not allow the events of it to stunt my personal growth. I had three daughters watching me and learning from me. I had to get it together. I had to establish (accept) myself on the inside. My titles (mom, daughter, friend, and nurse) had allowed me to hide behind the spirit of who I was, when I operated in each title. But it was in my quiet space where I felt the failure, the unworthiness and shame. In establishing who I am and whose I am in my mind firmly, I transformed my thoughts about myself.

I had a professor in college that stressed the fact that when we receive information in different forms (reading, writing, and listening) we can retain information much better and have better outcomes. This is a concept that I incorporated into my daily life. Using positive affirmations, listening to positive speakers, and finding someone to express myself to, along with eating and exercising, helped me to develop a positive way of thinking. In the bible, the book of Romans speaks about being transformed through the renewing of your mind. I had to retrain my mind and thought process as it pertained to ME. In one of the previous chapters we performed an assessment of ourselves to gain insight of the source or sources of the negative labels in our life. Now we will gain tools my performing a **S.E.L.F.** check. In performing the **S.E.L.F.** check we will be able to build self-confidence and establish ourselves as the person that we were predestined to become.

The **S.E.L.F.** check includes:
1. Saying Affirmations/ Pray throughout your day.
2. Exercise and Eat balanced meals
3. Listen to positive content.
4. Find someone that you can trust to share your thoughts with. (This person does not have to be a professional. If you feel that you may need the assistance of a professional, please seek the medical advice of a qualified professional.)

In performing the steps in the **S.E.L.F.** check, I changed the self-talk from a negative conversation to a positive one. The first check of saying positive affirmation and praying throughout the day was a key factor in firmly establishing who I am. The Merriam Webster dictionary provides one definition of affirmation as a positive and confident statement of fact or belief. I would write positive quotes on small note pads and place those on the mirrors around my home. One that I looked at daily read, "It does not matter how I got here. I'm here…that's all that matters! Love yourself!" This note reminded me to focus on the present, the past has already happened and I had to love myself period. I had many other affirmations, like "YOU, were created for a time such as THIS…" or a bible verse, "Trust in the Lord with all your heart, lean not to your own understanding, but in all your ways acknowledge Him and He will make your path straight." Prov. 3:5-6 This helped me tremendously and I believe that you would benefit from this practice. All it takes is time, small note pad, possibly tape, a pen and positive quotes. Once you have decided the quotes that you want to use, write them down on the note pads. Then place the notepads in areas of your home or room that will allow you the ability to read the affirmation daily. I placed my affirmation notes on the mirror in my bedroom. My daughter placed a few note affirmations in the medicine cabinet. I know someone else that placed their affirmations on the door of their closet. It does not matter where you place them, the only thing that matter is that the affirmations are read daily.

Our inner thoughts can make a direct effect on our physical body, with the task of getting ourselves to a positive way of thinking. We must provide our bodies with the proper amount of exercise and diet, which is the second **S.E.L.F.** check. What we ingest directly influences the way we feel about ourselves. How many times have you eaten a pizza and had one too many slices? What did you say to yourself once you felt full and stuffed with pizza? I can honestly say that the words that I have used to describe myself after I have stuffed myself, are not words that are positive and nice. I have literally said to myself, "OMG, I am so FAT. I am such a glutton. I am so disgusted with myself." Eating too many slices of pizzas caused me to talk negatively about myself and lead me to feeling bad about myself. During the time of establishing yourself, it would be best to incorporate eating a balanced meal and exercise into your routine.

Providing our bodies with the proper amount of exercise and rest, along with an adequate diet will assist in providing mental clarity. Renewing your mind to think differently requires energy and a balanced diet, along with exercise and rest, which are key in providing the necessary energy. I gave up carbonated drinks and incorporated more water into my daily regimen. I also started to cook more often. This required planning my weeks out and working my cooking schedule around my life schedule. When I visited restaurants, I would select healthier foods off the menu. It was not easy, and there were moments when I was not as compliant as I should have been. So, if you find yourself not complying to eating a balanced diet, exercise, and resting on a regular basis, do not beat yourself up over it. Start off slow pick one to incorporate into your lifestyle. If you relapse to the old behavior, start from where you left off and begin a new day with a fresh start!

The third task of the **S.E.L.F**. check is to listen to positive content. When I was going through my divorce I noticed that I was listening to a lot of sappy love songs. I would listen to them over and over. I would watch a bunch of romantic movies. I was obsessed with watching videos on relationships and how to make them work. One day while watching one of the relationship videos, I had a light bulb moment, you know one of those moments of clarity. The speaker on the video said, "you have to stop rehearsing the pain of your past so that your present can heal and your future can be positive." I do not even recall the name of the speaker that I was listening to at the time, but that one statement woke me up to what I was doing to myself. I was rehearsing the pain of my past by watching all of these romantic movies and listening to the love songs from my past. I was dwelling in the woulda, coulda, shoulda of my past as well.

I had to change some things up when it came to what I was listening to and watching. I began to find songs about strength and moving forward. I started to watch videos on self-love and healing. I even recorded my own voice to hear the positive affirmations in my own words. While watching one of the pastors on television, preach one of his Sunday sermons about forgiveness, I had a transforming moment. It was like the message was tailored just for me. I had to forgive myself.

Establishing myself included forgiveness. Not only forgiving others, but I had to forgive Mechel for allowing the negative label that I had placed in my mind, to hinder my personal growth. Outwardly, it seemed as though I had it all together. I had a great career as a nurse, wonderful daughters who were loving and respectful. To others, I had things all together, I was handling my new life with ease. In all reality I was stuck in the past of "What WOULDA happened if...", or "What COULDA been done differently if..." and "I SHOULDA done this..." I had become a prisoner to my own thoughts of my past. Those thoughts caused me to remain stagnant in personal growth. Along with the label of SHAME, was the label of FAILURE, and UNWORTHINESSS. One label was attached to the other and they were worn around my neck like a family heirloom necklace. I had taken ownership of those titles. In forgiving myself, I could release these self-placed titles from my identity.

If I had remained in the place of listening to the love songs, watching the romantic movies, and listening to the speakers who only talked about relationships, I would have remained stuck in my past. I had to change what I was listening to on a regular basis. Your situation may be different from mine. You may be listening to content that is perfect for your situation but ask yourself the question, "Am I healing from listening to this content or am I rehearsing the pain from my past? How do I feel after listening to the content?" A simple change in the content of what you are listening to, can change the way your think and feel about yourself.

The **S.E.L.F.** check also includes talking with someone that you can confide in, about your feelings and thoughts. Someone that you can trust. This person may be a family member or friend, but it needs to be someone that will allow you to vent and talk about where you are in life without any judgement, and sometimes without any opinion of what you are saying. In verbalizing your emotions and thoughts, you will give yourself the opportunity to hear your own voice speak your truth. And it will also allow you the opportunity to release what you have been carrying around. Holding on to the negative thoughts that we have about ourselves can cause stress, and many times that stress can cause health issues to develop. In releasing those thoughts when talking to your chosen confidant, you allow the freedom and healing t began.

Some may need to talk to a professional, such as a therapist or counselor. It is perfectly fine for you to reach out to someone that is an expert in listening and talking to people about their emotional and mental health. Sometimes when we are sick, we may take the suggestion of our friends and family on what medications to take to help us fight a cold. We take over counter medications, drink the orange juice and eat the soup that they recommend, but sometimes that cold may require us to take something stronger. At that point we may need to take an antibiotic or a prescribed medication that only a healthcare provider can prescribe. This will require us to make a doctor's appointment and go into be seen by a professional that can help us heal and feel better. The same is true when it comes to our mental and emotional health and accepting ourselves.

If you feel that talking to someone who you do not know on a personal level is something that you cannot do, then think of it as going to the doctor for a physical check up for a new patient appointment. You know nothing about the healthcare provider, but you are possibly about to expose yourself physically during the exam. They will take blood for labs, ask questions about your eating, sleeping and drinking habits. They are going to be all up in your business and you do not know them on a personal level, but you are trusting them with your body. Same thing goes when we reach out to a professional about our mental health. We are going to expose ourselves emotionally, but it is required in order for healing to take place. The end goal is healing and acceptance of ourselves. So, if you have a stigma as it concerns mental health, be open to the possibilities that can come from talking to someone that is neutral as it concerns our situation.

Performing the **S.E.L.F.** check is not a step by step tool. You do not have to perform each step in chronological order. If you want to focus on eating and exercising before you start to say words of affirmation or find someone to confide in before you listen to positive content, that is perfectly ok. These are tools that helped me along the way in establishing (accepting) myself fully. In following these tools, I hope that you gain the healing that you need to love yourself completely and move forward in a positive manner.

❧Reflections❧

Chapter Five

Love Yourself

It has always been easier for me to show love to others before I think of showing myself love. In my mind I associated love only with others and not myself. I took myself for granted and just assumed that I knew that I loved me. I never purposefully expressed the love to myself, it was just a surface type of love. I say this because when you love someone you take the time to get to know that person and understand that person. You spend time with them and imagine how life will be with that person. At this point in my life, I had never done that with myself. I had never taken the time to get to know MECHEL.

My full name is Vernice Mechel Mitchell, everyone calls me by a different name. If you were from my childhood and grew up with my sisters and brothers, you knew me as Suzie. My sister said I reminded her of one of her teachers and her first name was Suzie…I know it is a crazy way of having a name attached to you. My friends called me Chel and my parents called me Mechel. Throughout grade school I would have my friends call me Chel, like my friends from my neighborhood called me. Sometimes in school, I would get tired of having to explain to the teachers that I did not go by my first name, and I would prefer to be called by my middle name, so some of my old classmates know as Vernice. I grew up not liking the name Vernice. I really do not know why, I just did not like it. When I began to work, I would have my manager change my name tag to say "Mechel" instead having my first name on it. I would verbally say "I do not like that name, VERNICE!"

One day while praying and saying one of my affirmations, I gained clarity of what I was doing to myself. I constantly said to myself that I did not like the name that I had been given at birth. I knew that the bible spoke of how a person's name described who they were or who they belonged to. By me stating that I did not like my name, I was possibly subconsciously letting myself know that I did not like me. This was another light bulb moment for me. I was sabotaging myself with negative self-talk and I did not even realize that I was doing it. I was just talking about the name in itself, VERNICE, but who was Vernice? ME! I told myself over and over that I do not like ME! Yes, self-talk is

THAT serious and sensitive. Our subconscious sometimes has a way of only picking up certain things in conversation.

My intention was focused on my actual name, "I do not like the NAME, Vernice, but I only internalized as "I DO NOT LIKE…VERNICE." In saying that I did not like my name, I was basically saying that I did not like myself. I had placed the label of UNLOVED on myself and at that moment I realized that my thoughts about myself were not very loving. If I really thought about it, I was not very kind in the talk that I gave myself on a regular basis. I would often allow fear and doubt to stop me from doing things that I really wanted to do for myself. I would also put the goals and dreams of others before I would focus on my own. I did not put myself first and this was a way of saying that I was UNLOVED by ME!

Loving yourself is more than just words, it is an action as well. When we put the dreams and goals of others, like a significant other or family member's, before our own for a substantial amount of time, it will make us start to feel bad about ourselves. The cycle of negative self-talk continues and the progression of feeling unloved continues. It is ok to be supportive of others who are taking steps toward their goals and dreams, especially if it is your spouse or child. It is when we permanently place our own goals and dreams on the back burner, that we must do something differently. When we make goals for ourselves and do not complete them, it will sometimes leave a void in us, that will cause us to always feel like we shorted our personal growth and did not become who we were created to become.

The book of Matthew, chapter 22 and verse 39, Jesus informs us that the second greatest commandment of the Law is to "Love your neighbor as yourself." For some it is hard to love others because they have not learned to love themselves. For others, it is easier to love others because they have not taken the time to love themselves. They give and show love to others throughout their day, but they are empty on the inside. Then there are those who have a hard time showing love to other's because they do not love themselves. They are doing the commandment that Jesus left behind, they are loving their neighbor as themselves. Some cannot give what they do not have inside of them. I cannot give love when I do not have love of self.

Showing myself love, required me to be real with the one person that I could not avoid, and that was ME. I had to get to know myself. In getting to know me, I discovered that I really like me, and want the best for myself. I had muffled my dreams and goals by allowing fear of the unknown to overwhelm my thoughts. In the past I would tell myself that I could not do "it" because I had no experience in "it". Whatever the "it" was, I had talked myself out of it before the thought had a chance of becoming a reality. The label of DOUBT became a continued part of my self-talk. My "it' was nursing school. I had no idea of how to balance school and family. I did not know how I would pay for college and my household as well. I did not know if I would be a good nurse. I had gone through every bad scenario about attending nursing school in my mind. During the time of getting to know myself, I realized that I had stunted my own growth and buried my own dreams and goals. I had to change the way I thought about my own life.

I thought that by pampering myself from time to time with a massage or pedicure was showing myself love, but it is not the only way. Expressing love to yourself also includes educating yourself, eating/exercising regularly, investing in yourself and your future. I was one of those people that refused to pay X amount of dollars to attend any conference or I would only purchase books if they were on sale. I would not want to pay to take a refresher course or workshop, and there was no way that I was going to give up my hard-working money to take a class. I was not looking at those things as a way of showing myself love. I had to change the way I was thinking about taking the workshop, purchasing the book, or attending the class; these things are all investments. I had to look at them as an investment in myself. Showing love to yourself is doing things to improve yourself and your thoughts about yourself. Self-love is self-preservation. Loving yourself is like the oxygen that we breath and the food that we provide to our bodies for nourishment. Self-love includes doing things for yourself. Think of the stock market. You give your money to the stock broker to invest in hopes of obtaining a great return of money. When we invest in ourselves we show ourselves that we believe in ourselves enough to invest our own money in a class, a book, a mentor, a workshop or webinar that will help you reach your goals and dreams.

Go deeper when it comes to yourself. Do not just live a day to day routine life. Take a chance on the most important person in your life, YOU! Follow your dreams, set goals, and make the investment in yourself to show love. Its ok to go get your hair styled or to purchase a new pair of shoes to show love to your outer appearance and satisfy yourself temporally. Remember that self-love includes moving forward towards your own dreams and goals. Investing in yourself is a great way to express self-love. Go ahead and love on yourself...it is ok to invest in you!

❧Reflections❧

Chapter Six

Share

The way we feel towards ourselves can have a direct effect on the way we view and treat the people in our lives. The negative thoughts that we have about ourselves will often times stop us from allowing others to get too close in fear that they may recognize the "real" person inside. The negative label(s) that we have carried around for years become a way of sheltering ourselves, and we become isolated from others. This behavior halts us from connecting with other people and eventually hinders our personal growth. We can get so wrapped up in our own negative thoughts about ourselves, that we began to think that no one will want to be around us, or we believe that no one will be interested in what we have experienced. We become trapped in our own negative mind-set and sharing with others becomes more and more difficult.

My experience from sharing my thoughts and experiences with others has not only helped me through the healing process, but I have noticed that others have found healing in themselves just from me sharing my own experiences. When we can share our experiences with others and truly be transparent, it allows the other person an opportunity to relate to our experience. We often hear people talk about "keeping it real" and that usually comes when they are trying to expose someone else or prove a point to someone else. When we "keep it real" about our own life and truly have healed from our past, those experiences will lose strength in our lives and we are able to speak on those things from a place of healing and strength, instead of a place of pain and stress.

For many years, I carried around the pain of an experience that I had in my early adolescent years. I was ashamed of the stigma that I would possible have if I had shared it with anyone that I knew. I hid it deep down inside of myself, with the hopes of never having to face it ever again. I was given the label of being "hot," and was told that I was acting grown at an early age, so when this happened to me I was not shocked. In my mind I was just living up to be who I was already told that I was growing up. I was a young girl whose mind was being manipulated by someone that was much older than her. I was twelve and he was nineteen, he may have been older than that at the time but that was the age that he told me. I remember that I had only just turned twelve years old.

He was like a predator that watched his prey on a daily basis. He lived on the same street as the candy store, so I would walk by every day, and he would be there daily. He would tell me how pretty I was and compliment my body. He would say all kinds of things to show that he was interested in me. He was in my head. He got me to tell him all kinds of things about my life and my living situation. I was too young to even figure out that he was just casing me and telling me whatever my young mind needed to hear to feel comfortable around him. One day he asked me if he could walk me home and like a dummy I said he could. I didn't see anything wrong with it, what would be the harm with him walking me home. During the walk home, he gathered more details about my living situation and I naively answered each question without any hesitation. He was just gathering more and more intel about me.

At the time, my mom and sister had overlapping work schedules. My mom had to be at work at 11pm and my sister got off work at 11pm, so there would be about a thirty minute to one-hour window that I would be home alone. Guess who had this information...Mr. nine-teen years old. He was a con about how he manipulated my young mind. He had me convinced that he was looking out for my own wellbeing, when he asked if I wanted him to come over to the house to hang out with me, while I was home alone. I recall saying to him that I would be ok and I told him that my mom would never allow him to be there with me. His comeback was on point to my twelve-year-old mind. He told me that he was concerned about me and could not be at his house knowing that I was home alone for any amount of time. He was concérned about my wellbeing and I thought that was the sweetest thing for him to be thinking about me. At this point, he had me. I let him come over. He would wait until my mom would leave for work and stay until just before my sister would get home. Day after day for about a week, he would come over and he would never try anything with me. In my eyes, he was being a great friend that wanted to look out for my safety. When in all actuality he was just "casing" my living situation and monitoring the amount of time that I would be home alone. One day, the "friend" that was looking out for me, took it upon himself to take advantage of me. He took my innocence, all in such a short amount of time. I was left feeling empty and sad, but I also felt that it was my fault, and a life that I was destined to live up to because of the label that was placed on me.

There was no way that I could ever tell anyone about what happened to me, because he told me not to tell anyone. I also thought, who would believe that I did not want what he did to me to happen? During that time of my life, I was constantly told that I was acting hot and grown. I was accused of having sex, but really did not know what sex was at the time. To be honest, I did not understand it, after it happened to me. I was clueless. I knew that I did not like the feeling during the act and I did not like the way I felt afterwards. I was so naïve about sex, and the terms used to describe the act and the actions of it. I remember asking him to stop doing what he was doing to me and his answer was, "Hold on let me get one more nut in." My young brain did not know what the heck he was talking about. At that age, I knew that boys would refer to the testicles as "nuts," so I thought that he was placing his testicles inside me. I just laid there and allowed him to do whatever he wanted to me. I was left in pain and not knowing what to do or who to turn to at the time. So, I thought that I would just carry the shame and confusion around with me for the rest of my life. I was determined to take this secret with me to my death. I did not want anyone to know what happened to me, not because I felt that it was wrong, but because I felt I was just living up to labels that were placed on me. Who would believe me when I told them? I thought the act that was done to me was just something that was supposed to happen because I wore shorts that drew that kind of attention. I felt that I caused the attention to be drawn to me by the clothes that I wore. I did not realize that something wrong had even happened to me, in my mind I deserved it.

The labels that were placed on me as a child caused me to accept his behavior as my fault. The little girl inside me was muted for so many years. It was life experiences that gave me knowledge to understand that what was done to me was wrong. For years and years, the little girl inside of me was mourning the loss of her innocence. She wanted so bad for her voice to be heard. For someone, anyone to know that she did not like what happened to her and that she did not do anything to cause him to do that to her. It was not until I was in my middle thirties, only about ten years ago, when I felt the courage to share my experience with someone else.

It was difficult to share with someone else because I did not know how they would react, and part of me thought the blame would be placed on me for allowing it to happen. Sharing my story was not a planned event. Remember, I was planning on taking this to the grave with me. It was a moment when I was like, "The time is now." A spontaneous moment when I did not care what would be thought of me or who would blame me. I had taken the steps to heal the little girl inside of me from the labels that had been placed on her. In that moment I was giving her a space to speak her truth and not be left to think something was wrong with her. I gave the younger Vernice an opportunity to be free, so that healing could take place.

In sharing my experience with that special person, I allowed them to experience my vulnerable moment, and transparency allowed them to relate to my experience. This exchange between the two of us allowed the healing process to take place for us both, since my story was like her life story. When I opened myself to share my experience, she could relate and felt comfortable in expressing herself to me. The person that I had known for over a decade, had been carrying around a deep secret for so many years, just as I did. We had talked so many times about life, children, relationships and all kinds of things in our lives, but we had never shared this part of our lives. In that moment, I knew that healing takes place when we were transparent and shared our life experiences.

Sharing is not only for the "sharer" but also for the "sharee." We are not meant to walk this experience of life alone. We were created to relate to one another, and while in relationship with our fellow man we can assist each other in the healing process. Once we have taken the steps to heal from the negative labels of our past, we should take the steps to help others heal. Our experiences and our healing are not just for us to keep to ourselves. In sharing my story, I hope that you will be able to relate to my experiences and heal from the negative labels that you have carried inside over the years.

❧Reflections❧

Chapter Seven

Renew, Relabel, Repackage

Our actions are formulated in our mind. One thought that lasts a few seconds, can develop into a full-blown thought process that grows into an action plan for our lives. When we free ourselves of negative thinking, we have the opportunity to allow positivity to occupy that same space in our life. When we give power to the negative thoughts and labels, we ultimately halt our forward progression in personal growth. When we take the steps to change the way we think of ourselves, we have the opportunity for growth and can develop into our purpose. Mind renewal has to occur first in order for transformation to occur.

The person that once thought of themselves as the negative label, has the power to replace the label with a more positive one. The old label is shed when the person's mind is renewed. The individual can relabel themselves by replacing old negative self-thoughts, with positive thoughts and descriptions. Relabeling our thoughts will cause action to take place, and it will start to reflect in the way we carry ourselves and go about leading our lives. Our purpose will develop as we focus our minds and think of ourselves in a positive manner. Our thoughts become our actions. **A renewed mind allows us the opportunity to relabel your thoughts and repackage your life.**

The negative labels that were placed on me, made me feel like I was quicksand, stuck on the conveyor belt of life, with no real direction. I was going through the motions of life because I rehearsed the negativity over and over in my mind. On the outside, I seemed as though I had everything together. My children were happy and loved. I had a great career, great family and friends. I seemed to be ok, but deep inside I had negative thoughts about myself. I always desired to have more out of life, but the negative thoughts had me stuck in a box. I was living a life based off of fear and doubt. I had given power to the negative thoughts and hindered my own personal growth. I understood that my mind had to be renewed.

When I began to study the Word of God, I gained a better understanding of who I am, and who I belong to, I could release those negative labels by replacing them with what the Word said about me. I applied the Word of God to my life by making the descriptions personal. I understood the Word to be true and active in my life, because I had experienced God's grace and mercy on an intimate and spiritual level.

Jeremiah 1:5 states, "Before I formed you in the womb I knew you, before you were born I set you apart; I appointed you as a prophet of nations." When I read that, I cried. "Yes". If you recall from one of the previous chapters, I was the little girl that accepted the label of bastard. So, when I read this verse, it excited me to know that God knew me even before I was formed in my mother's womb. That was amazing to me! How could I go on thinking negatively about myself after reading that verse? There was no way that I could. God has always known me, and he loved me enough to set me apart, and appointed me as a prophet of nations. I had to renew the thoughts that I was having about myself so that I could walk into my purpose. I read and knew God to be my Father in Heaven, so there was no way that I could ever think of myself as a bastard. God had to show me that I also have an earthly father that loves me dearly and I was open to God renewing my mind as it concerned my relationship with him.

One day the phone rang, it was my father on the other end. During the conversation, we got on the subject of my birth, and out the of the blue my daddy said to me, "Mechel, do you know that I always wanted you? You were not an accident or mistake, you were made in love. I asked your mom to have you and she did." Tears rolled down my face. I was stunned, but not from the words that my dad spoke to me, but because of the love that God has for me. It was demonstrated in the conversation with my father. God knew that I needed to hear those words. I really did need to hear that from my earthly father. I listened to my dad talk and his words filled my heart with joy. I could no longer think of myself as a bastard child. Although, my parents were never married, I was wanted by my earthly father, but most importantly my heavenly Father. I thought differently of myself after the conversation with my dad. My father and I had always had an estranged relationship, but that conversation led up to our connection becoming more solidified.

In renewing my mind, I could relabel my thoughts and repackage my life. When I released the thought of being a bastard child from my mind, the thoughts about myself were changed and replaced with new, positive thoughts. Those thoughts fueled the way I interacted with my father, and our relationship was repackaged with the love of God. I was no longer stuck in that area of my life. The negative label had no power over my life anymore. I no longer wore the label of a bastard child or someone that was unwanted. From that point on I labeled myself as "SET APART."

The negative thoughts that I had about myself, caused me to live in fear, which placed limits on my life. The negative thoughts that came from labels, shame, and doubt, delayed my personal growth at different stages of my life. I carried the thoughts of shame and doubt around in my mind and at some points of my life I started to believe those things about myself. Sometimes the self-doubt would be so strong that I would talk myself out doing things that I really wanted to do. Instead of focusing on the many things that I did know how to do in life, I would always point out the things that I didn't know how to do.

I would disqualify myself before I even attempted to perform the task. Fear of the unknown had me paralyzed.

I was a Certified Medical Assistant(CMA) before I became a Registered Nurse. I always wanted to become a nurse, so people in my family were surprised when I quit my job to attend CMA school. I told my family that I had decided to attend school to become a CMA instead going nursing school to become a RN, because I wanted to see if I would really like working in healthcare. I was ashamed to say that I doubted my ability to become a Registered Nurse along with the doubt in my ability to juggle nursing school, family life, and a job. The negative thoughts about myself were hindering my progression in life.

During one of my study times, while reading Philippians 4:13, the answer was given to me clear as day. That scripture reads, "I can do ALL things through Christ who strengthens me." There it was, my answer to how I was going to remove the doubt and feeling of shame. God was going to give me strength to endure whatever obstacle I would encounter in school. I had to believe that I had the ability to do what God had placed before me to complete. I could accomplish this goal, not by my own strength, but the strength that Christ would provide to me when I needed it. Through prayer and meditation, God strengthened my spirit. The road to become a Registered Nurse was not a smooth ride, but it was one that was worth it. Doubt was replaced with BELIEF, CONFIDENCE replaced shame, and FAITH stood in the place of fear.

Renewing our minds, relabeling our thoughts and repackaging our lives is a continual process. The negativity will always want to occupy space in our lives, that is why we must always be on alert to recognize when our self-thoughts have become negative. When we can let go of the negative labels, assess our lives, be all that we can be, and establish and love ourselves, we become free from the pain of the negative self-thoughts. Sharing our experiences with others becomes a part of the healing process, when we feel free from the hurt that the negative label caused in our lives. We can connect with others who can relate to our experience, this connection becomes reciprocal. When you share your experience with someone else, it not only helps you has the person sharing, by giving you strength and healing, but it also is a way for the person hearing your experience to heal, when they can relate. Sharing our experiences, gives us power over the negative thoughts that would occur if we were to keep them to ourselves. Negative labels grow into negative thoughts when we do not take action to recognize the self-talk that we are giving ourselves. If those negative thoughts are not taken captive, they grow into a way of living that can stunt our personal growth. Take the time to listen to your thoughts about yourself, identify any negative labels, and apply the strategies that were shared in this book. Be healed, be free, move forward…You deserve it!

www.sow365daz.com

❧Reflections❧